DATE DUE			

ACTION SPORTS

SNOWBOARDING

KENNY ABDO

abdopublishing.com

Published by Abdo Zoom, a division of ABDO, P.O. Box 398166, Minneapolis, Minnesota 55439. Copyright © 2018 by Abdo Consulting Group, Inc. International copyrights reserved in all countries. No part of this book may be reproduced in any form without written permission from the publisher.

Printed in the United States of America, North Mankato, Minnesota.
092017
012018

**THIS BOOK CONTAINS
RECYCLED MATERIALS**

Photo Credits: Alamy, Icon Sportswire, iStock, Shutterstock
Production Contributors: Kenny Abdo, Jennie Forsberg, Grace Hansen
Design Contributors: Dorothy Toth, Neil Klinepier

Publisher's Cataloging-in-Publication Data

Names: Abdo, Kenny, author.
Title: Snowboarding / by Kenny Abdo.
Description: Minneapolis, Minnesota: Abdo Zoom, 2018. | Series: Action sports |
    Includes online resource and index.
Identifiers: LCCN 2017939271 | ISBN 9781532120961 (lib.bdg.) |
    ISBN 9781532122088 (ebook) | ISBN 9781532122644 (Read-to-Me ebook)
Subjects: LCSH: Snowboarding--Juvenile literature. | Winter Sports--
    Juvenile literature. | Extreme Sports--Juvenile literature.
Classification: DDC 796.939--dc23
LC record available at https://lccn.loc.gov/2017939271

TABLE OF CONTENTS

SNOWBOARDING

Snowboarding was invented in the 1960s. It was called snurfing, for "snow surfing."

Snowboarding involves moving down a snow-covered hill while standing on a board. The board is attached to the rider's feet.

BOARDS

A snowboard is a flat board with curved edges and **bindings**. The bindings hold the rider's feet in place.

Most snowboards are made from a combination of **fiberglass**, wood, plastic, and metal.

Snowboarders can ride **regular** or **goofy** footed. A rider's **dominant** foot should always be in back.

Riders must maintain their
balance. This takes a lot of
practice. Falling is a part
of learning.

COMPETITION

The sport of snowboarding made its **Olympic** debut in 1998 in Nagano, Japan.

Snowboarders compete in halfpipe and the giant **slalom** events. A halfpipe is a U-shaped ramp built into the snow.

Shaun White is considered the best snowboarder in the world. He holds the record for highest score in men's halfpipe at the Winter **Olympics**.

GLOSSARY

bindings – a piece that connects a boot to the snowboard.

dominant – the most powerful or influential.

fiberglass – a material made of plastic and very fine fibers of glass.

goofy – standing on a board with your right foot forward.

Olympics – the biggest sporting event in the world that is divided into summer and winter games.

regular – standing on a board with your left foot forward.

slalom – downhill snowboarding between poles and gates.

ONLINE RESOURCES

Booklinks
NONFICTION NETWORK
FREE! ONLINE NONFICTION RESOURCES

To learn more about snowboarding, please visit abdobooklinks.com. These links are routinely monitored and updated to provide the most current information available.

INDEX